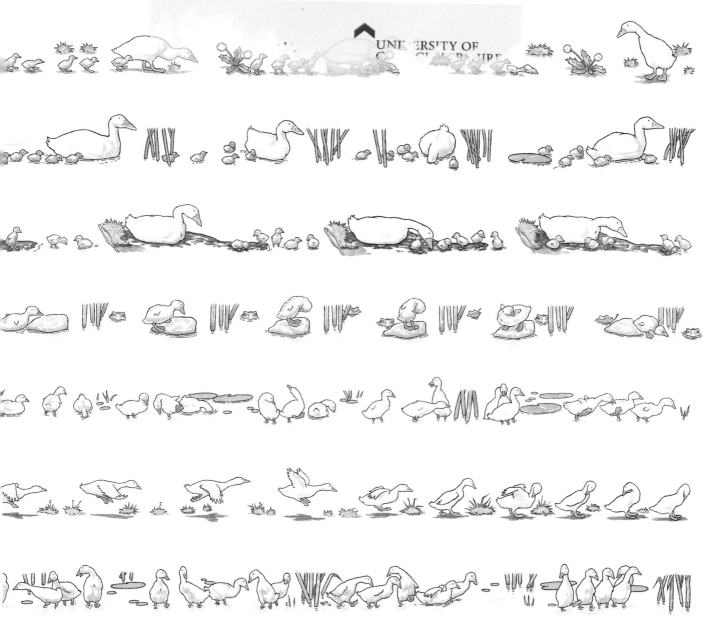

**A DORLING KINDERSLEY BOOK**

**Written and edited by** Angela Royston
**Art Editor** Nigel Hazle
**Production** Marguerite Fenn
**Illustrator** Rowan Clifford

First published in Great Britain in 1991 by
Dorling Kindersley Limited, 9 Henrietta Street, London WC2E 8PS

Reprinted 1991, 1993, 1994

A CIP catalogue record for this book is available
from the British Library

ISBN 0-86318-545-2

Typesetting by Goodfellow & Egan
Colour reproduction by Scantrans, Singapore
Printed in Italy by L.E.G.O.

# SEE HOW THEY GROW
# DUCK

photographed by
# BARRIE WATTS

DK

DORLING KINDERSLEY
London • New York • Stuttgart

# In the nest

My mother has laid her eggs in this
nest. She sits on them to keep
them warm.

Inside each egg a new duckling
is growing. This one is me. I am just
beginning to hatch.

# Just hatched

I have chipped
away my shell
and now I am
pushing myself out.

At last I am out of my egg.

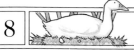

I can see and hear and stand
and walk. I can cheep
too. Where is
my mother?

# First swim

I am two days old now. I am going to the pond for my first swim.

As soon as I am in the water, I start to swim.

I use my webbed feet to push me through the water.

# Feeding

I am seven days old and getting bigger. I like to explore new things.

This bowl has wet mud in it.
I search the mud with my
beak for things to eat.

Now I've jumped right into the bowl.

# In the water

I dabble in the water for things to eat.

I am two weeks old and I love to swim in the water.

I shake the water off my feathers.

# New feathers

I am three weeks old.
My yellow down is
falling out and new
white feathers are
beginning to grow.

I stay close to the other ducklings.
Our mother watches out for danger.

Sometimes we huddle together. Our untidy feathers help to keep us warm.

# Nearly grown up

I am six weeks old and nearly
grown up.

All my feathers are white and my wings are bigger and stronger.

See how much I have grown. This bowl is small now, but it seemed big when I first jumped into it.

# See how I grew

The egg

One hour old

Two days old  Seven days old  Two weeks old

Three weeks old

Six weeks old

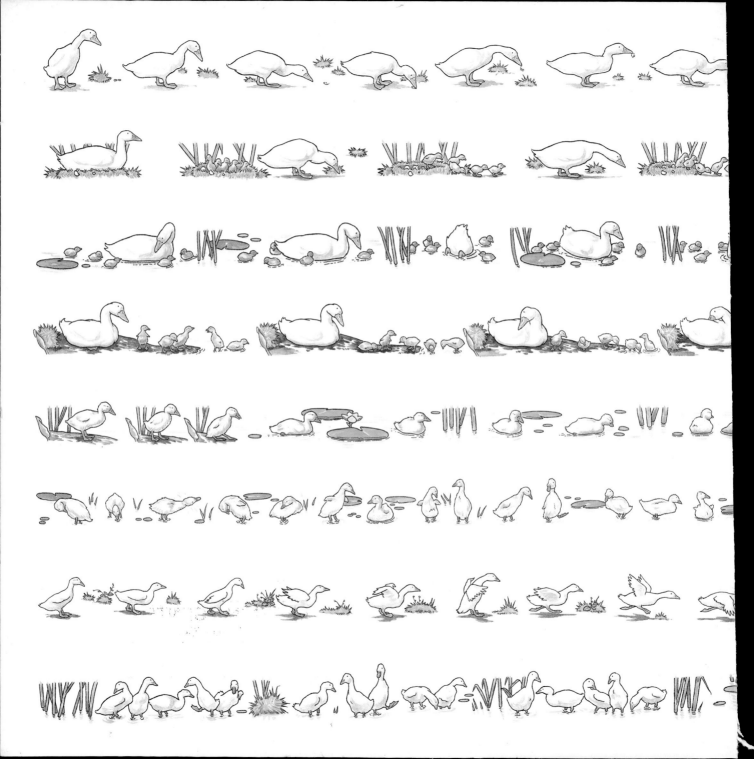